Lion

Pig

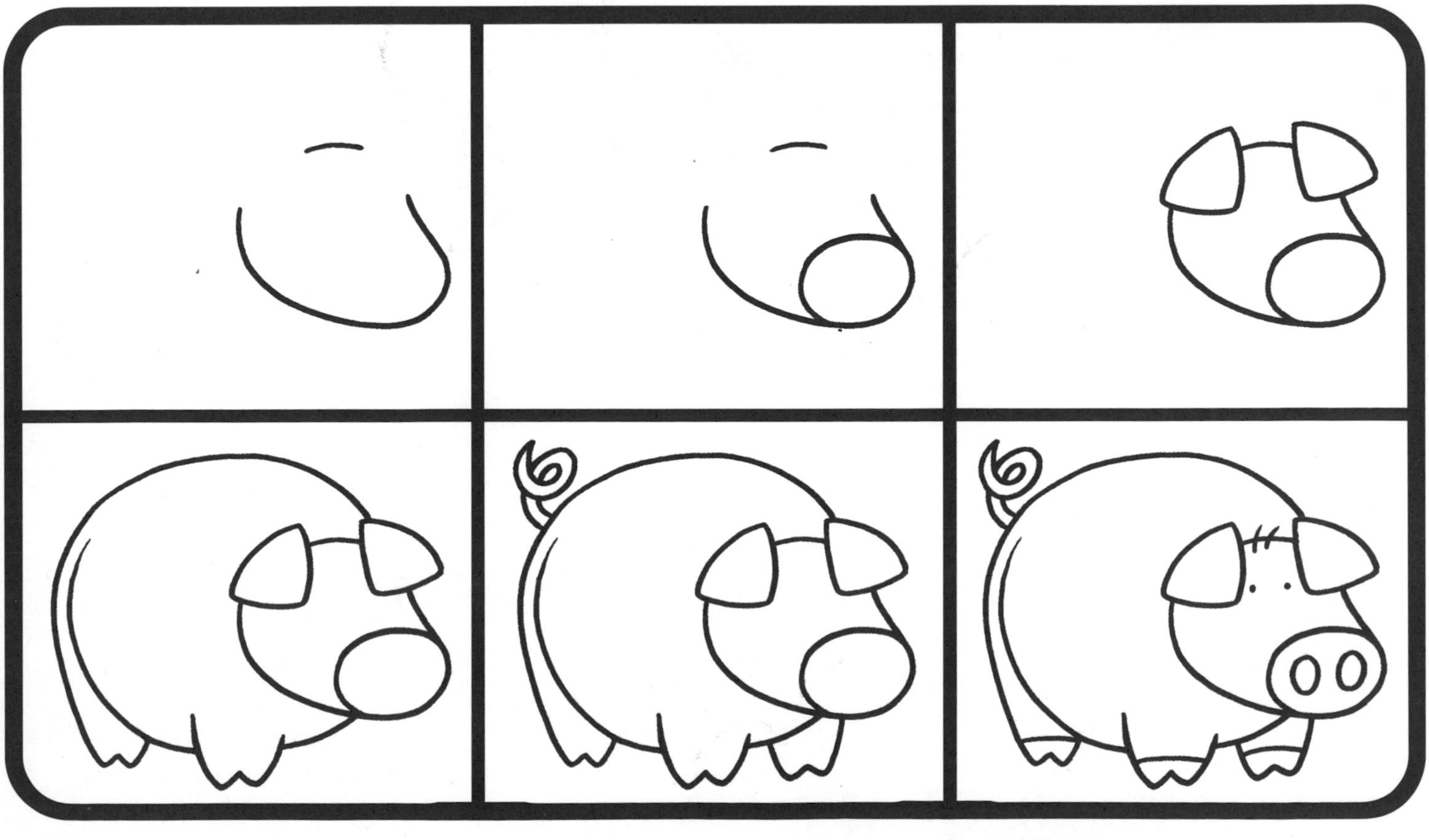

Lobster

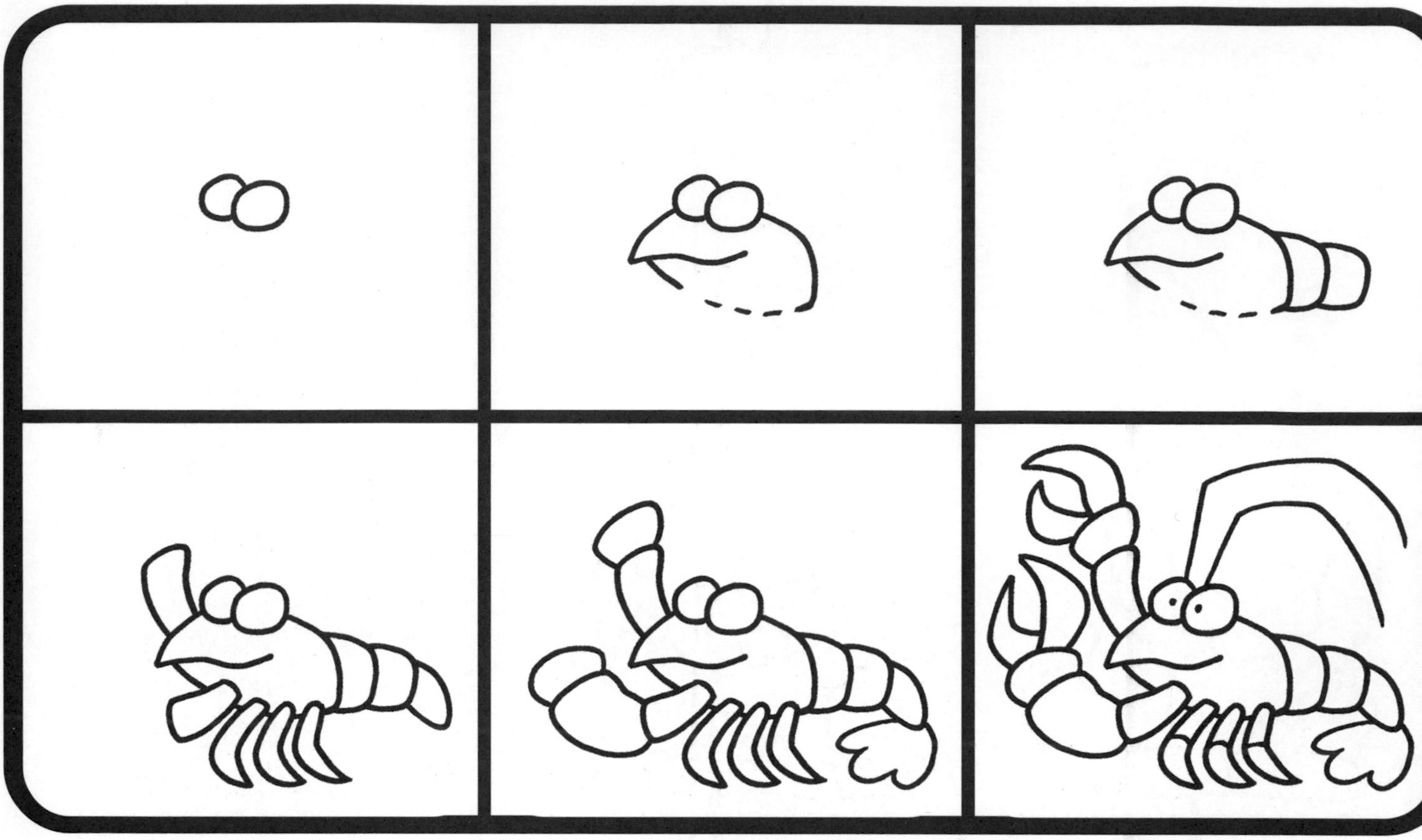

Kangaroo

Eagle

Chimpanzee

Cat

Turtle

Dog

Baboon

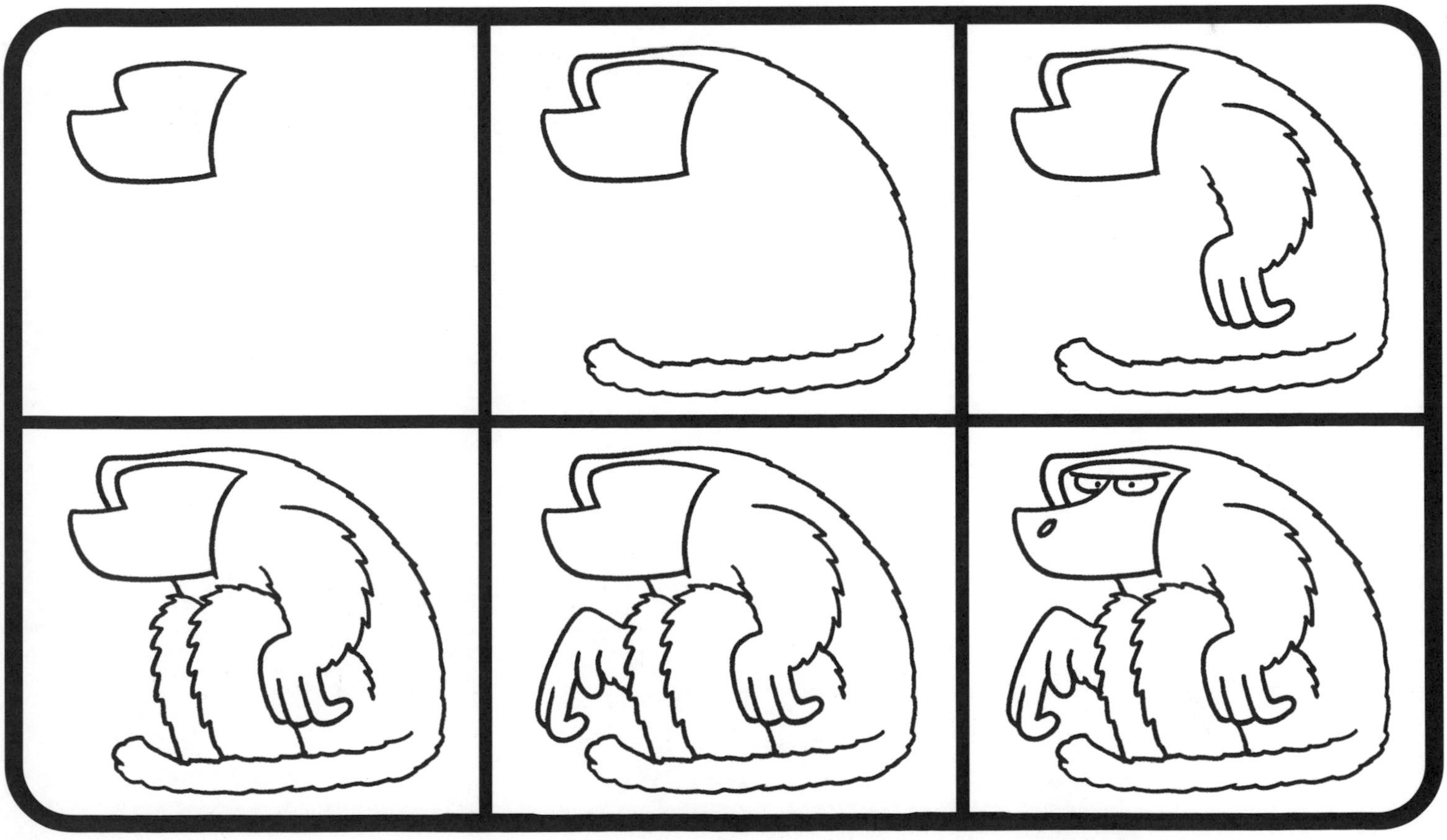

Fish

Tiger

Hedgehog

Kiwi

Parrot

Stag Beetle

Anteater

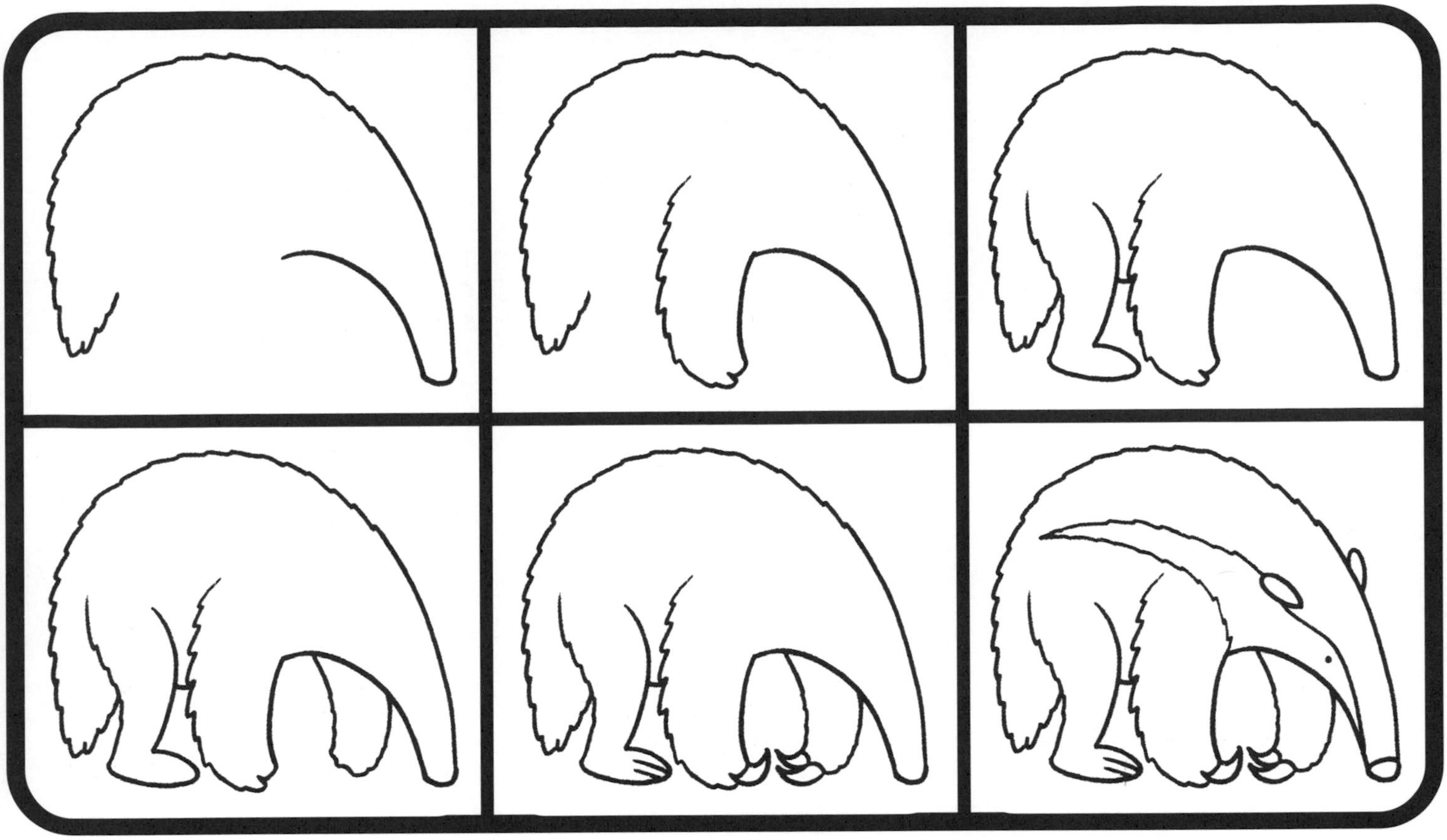

Chicken

Budgie

orang-utan

Rhino

Bat

Squirrel

Donkey

Toad

owl

Crab

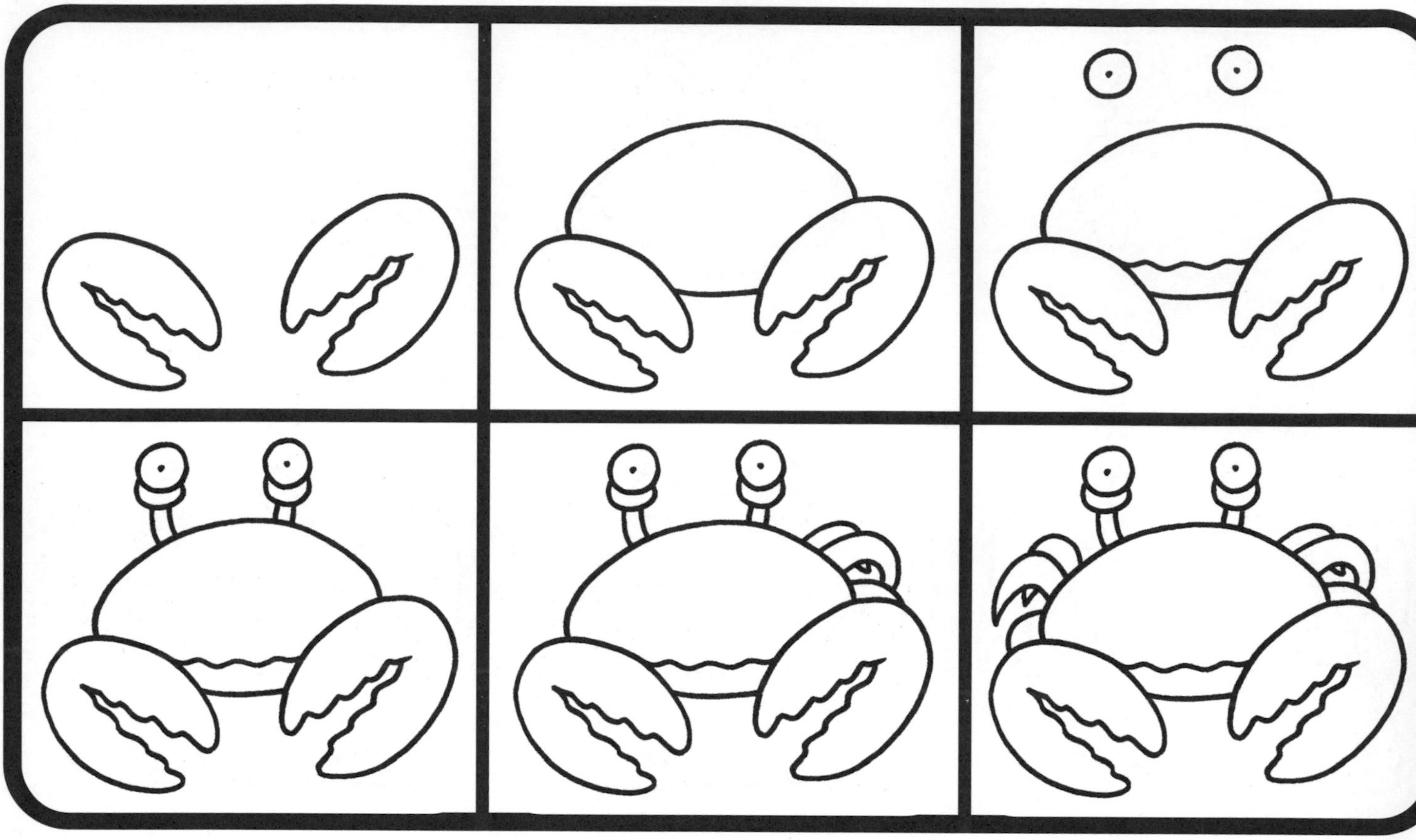

Dolphin

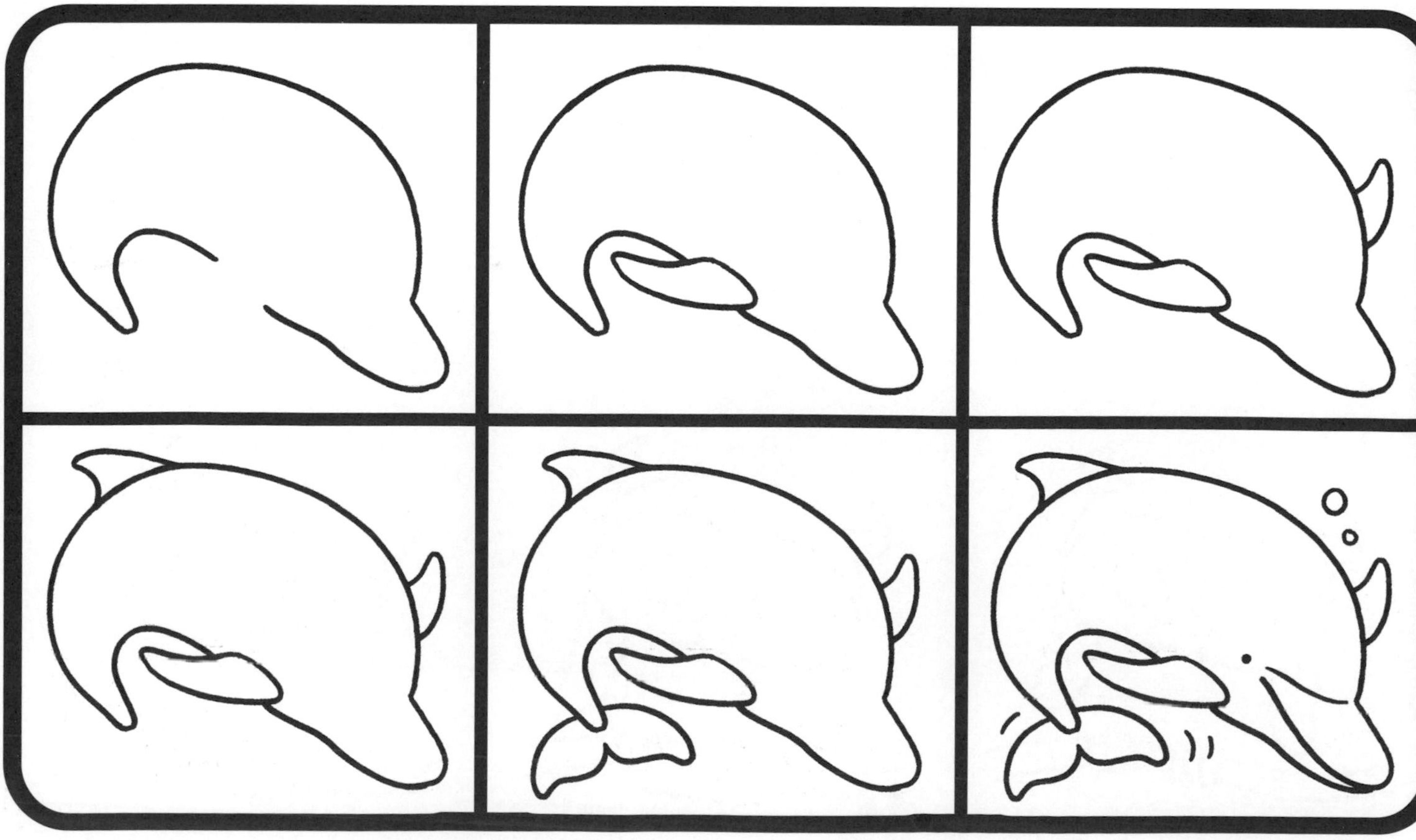

Cow

Rat

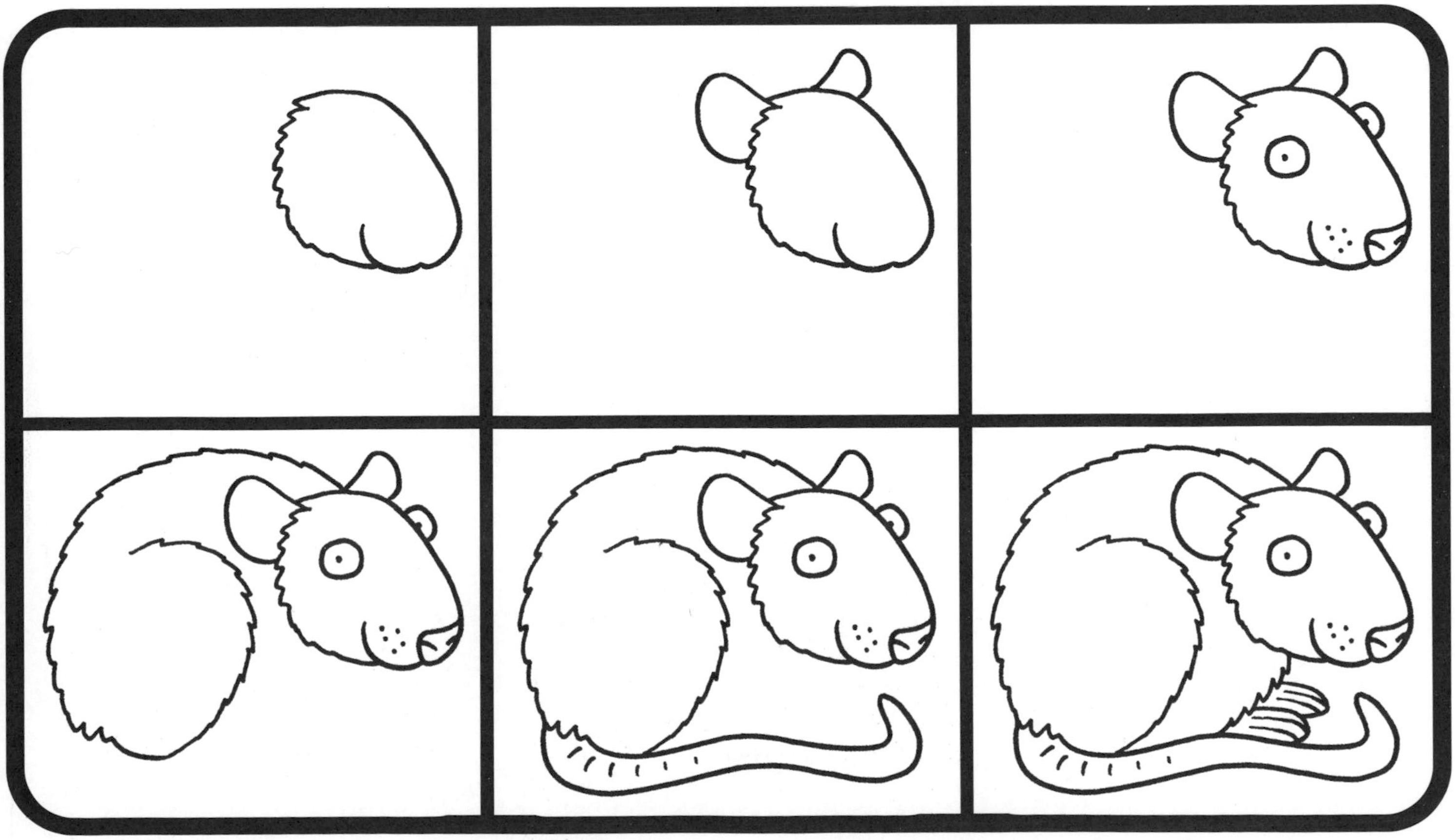

Seal

Tortoise

Camel

Ant

Peacock

Jellyfish

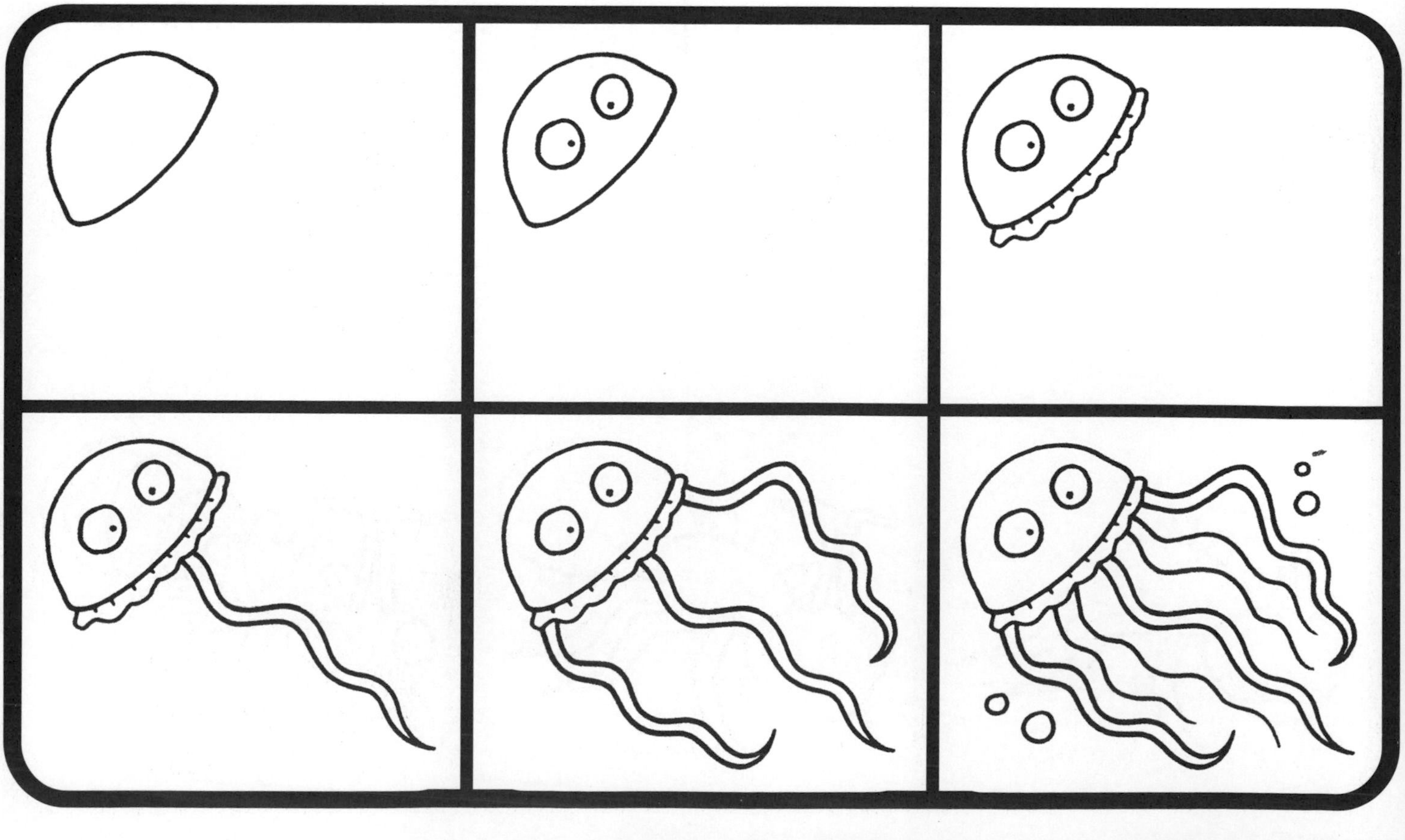

otter

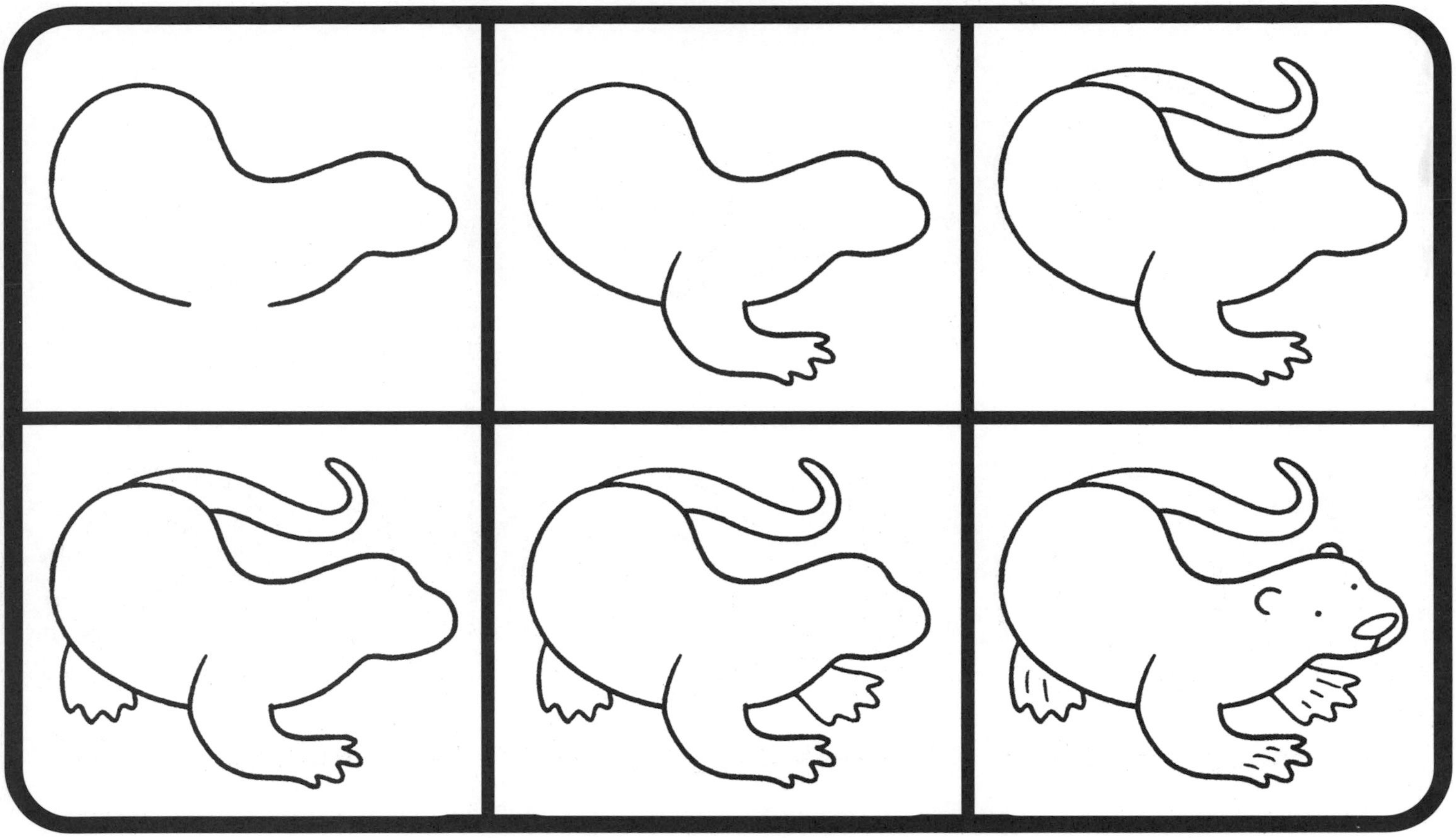

Zebra

Snail

Chameleon

Rabbit

Sheep

Panda

Snake

orca

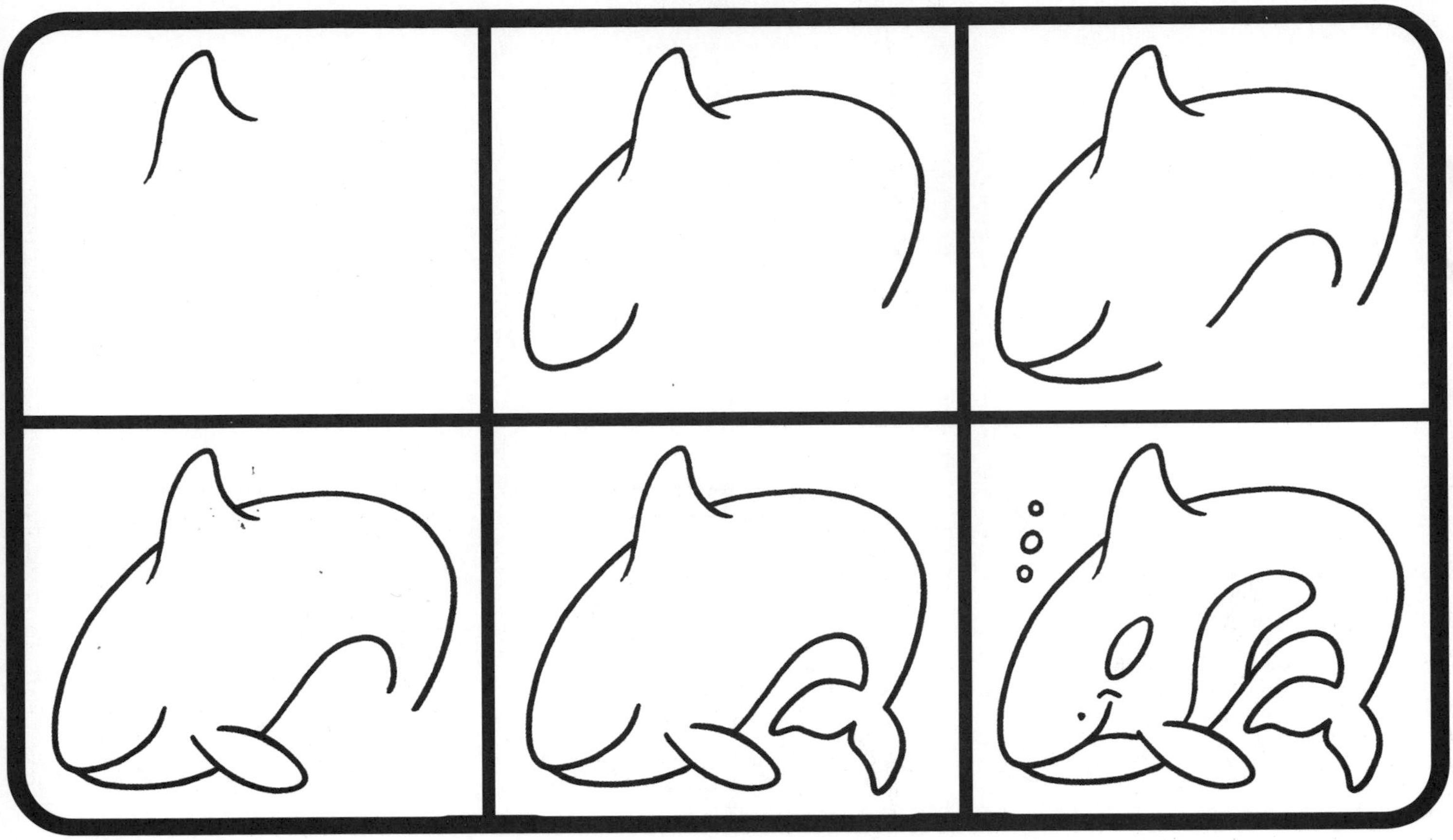

Toucan

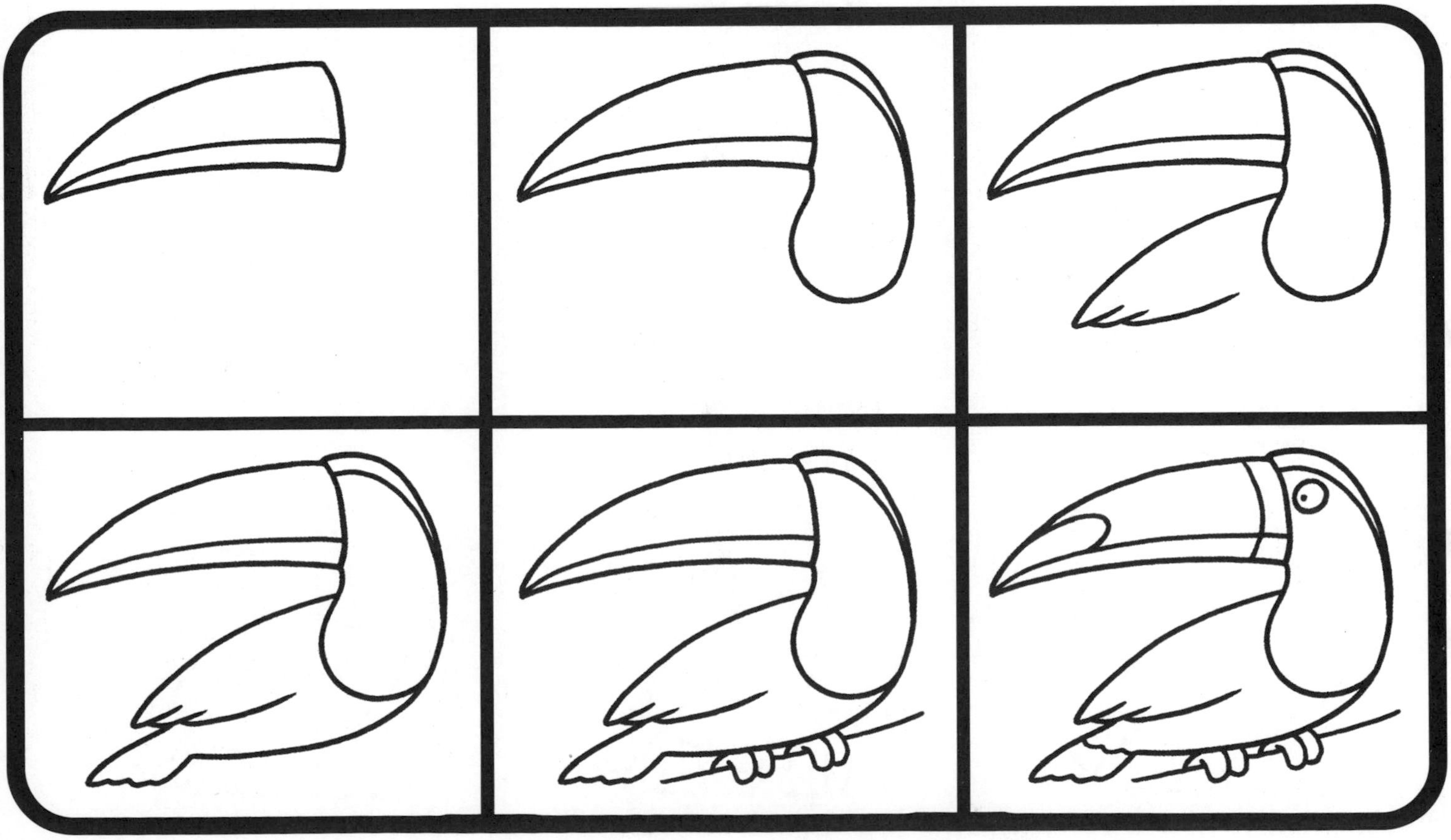

Lemur

Bison

Horse

Penguin

Elephant

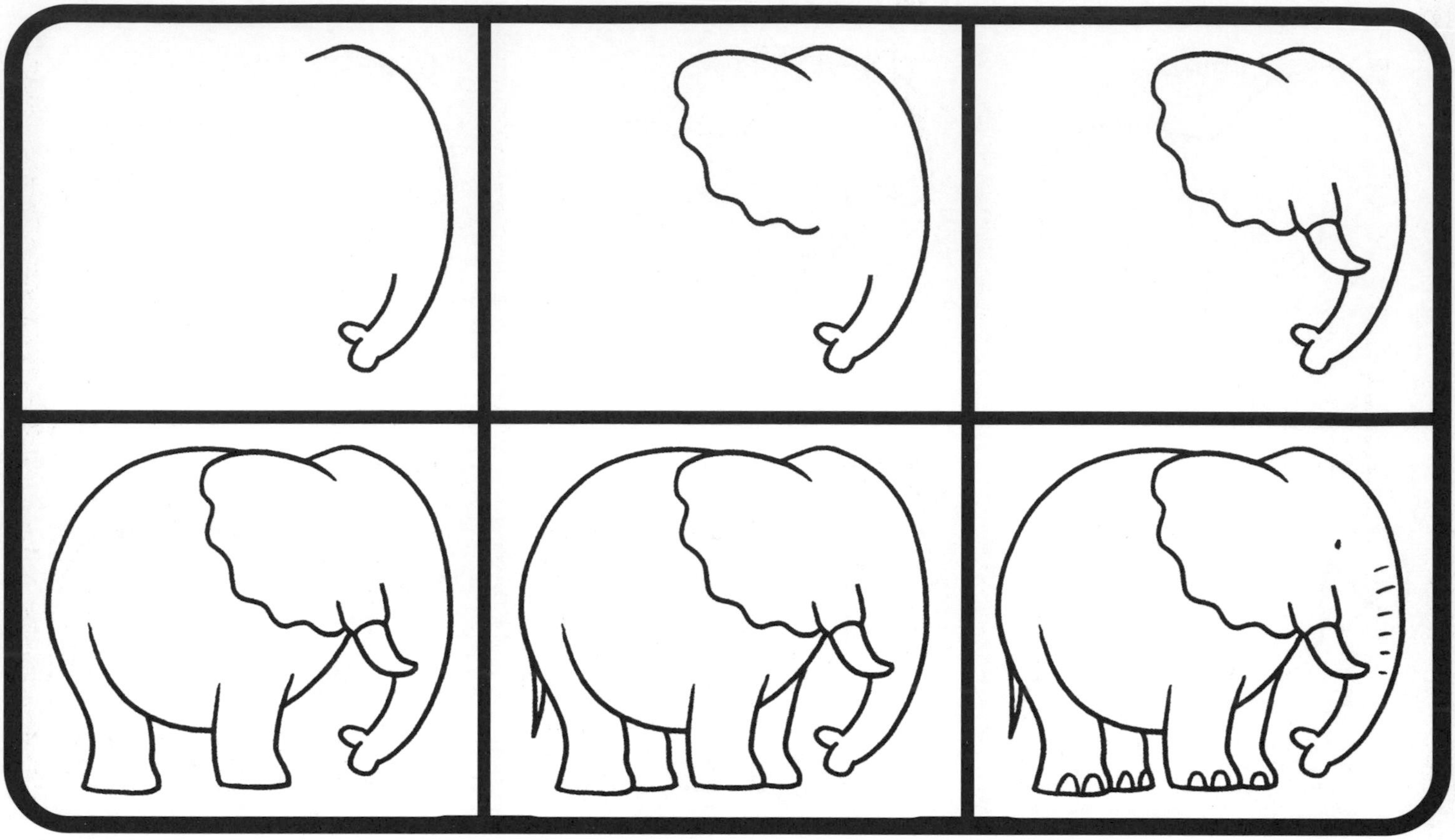

Frog

Shark

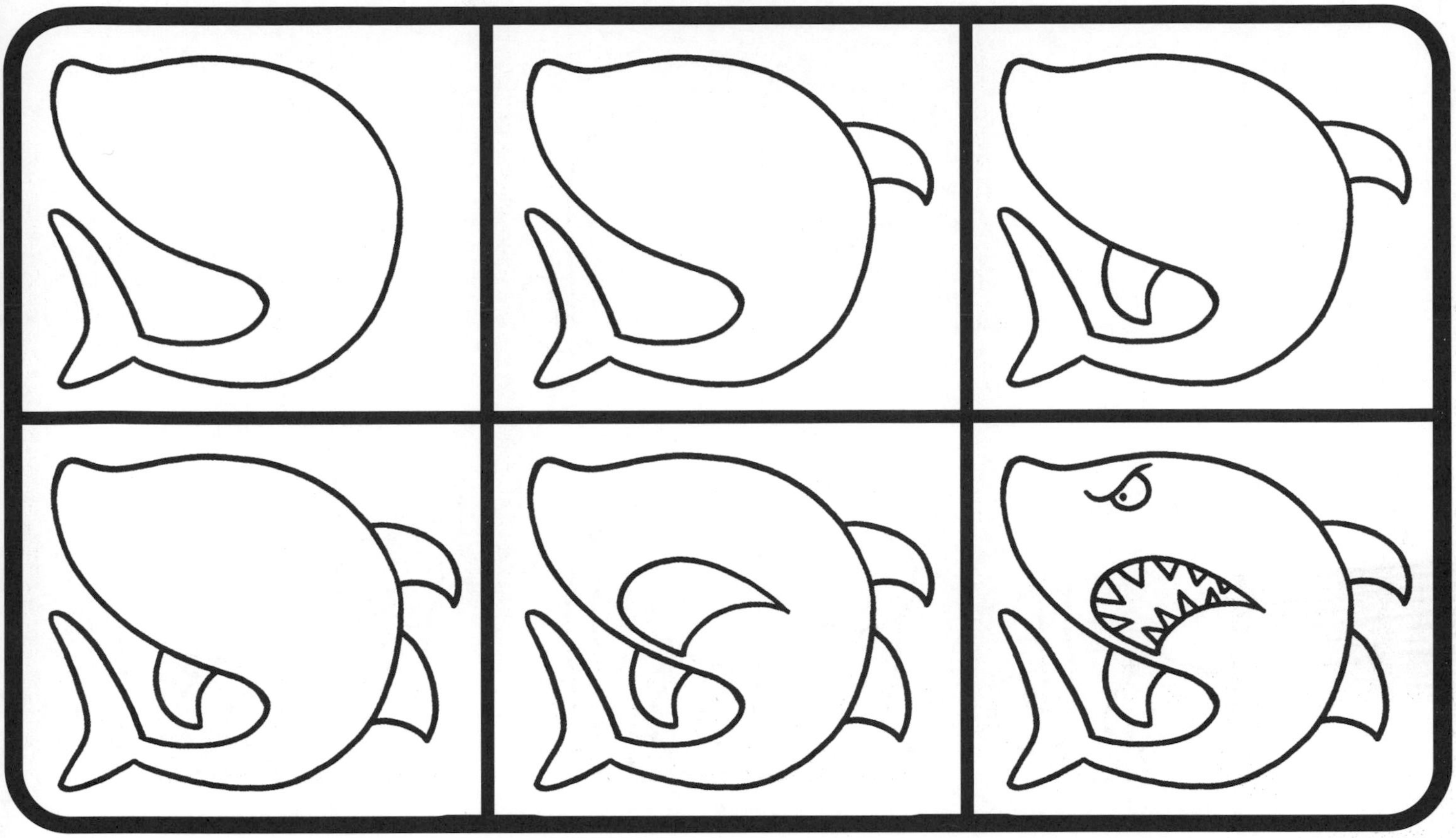

Goat

Panther

Kingfisher

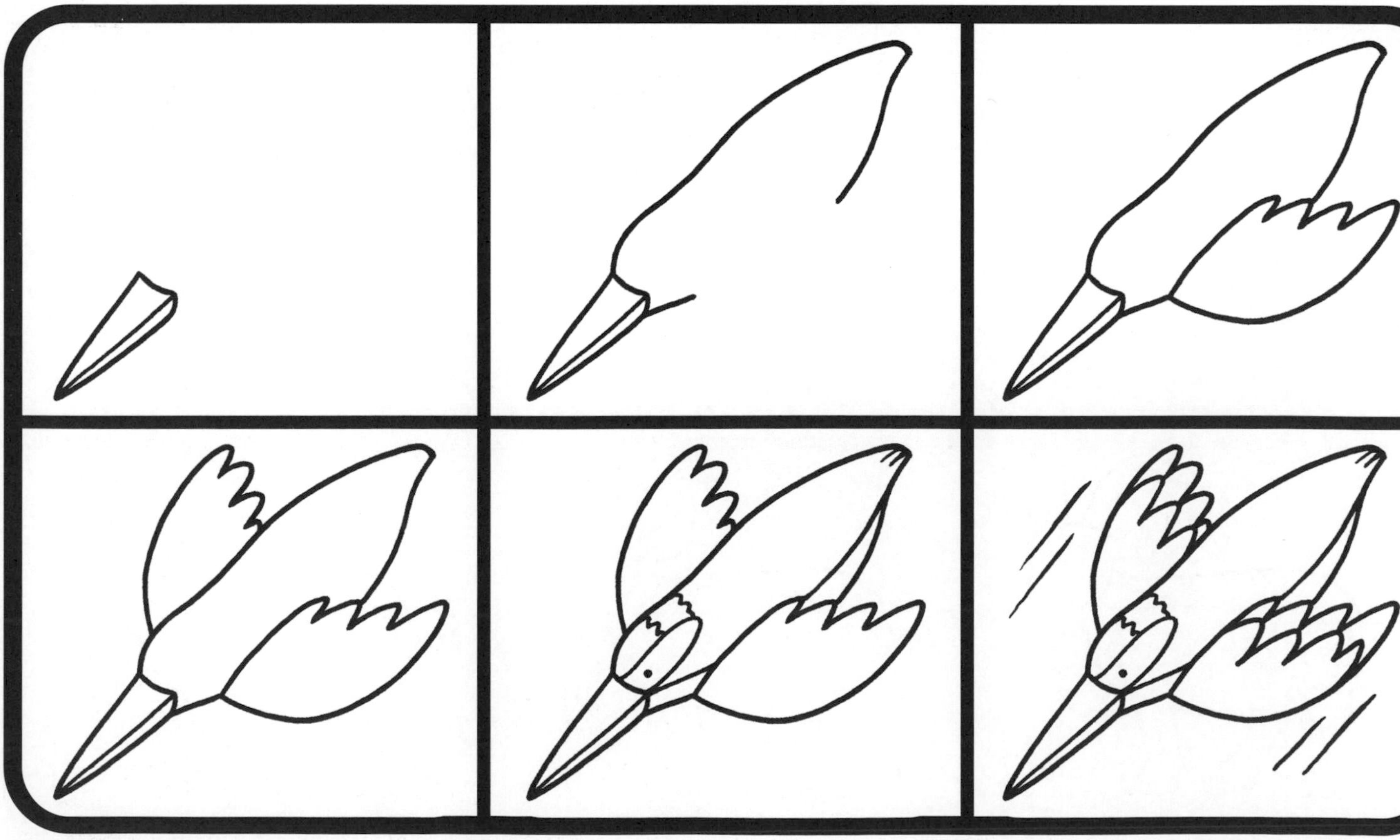

Grasshopper

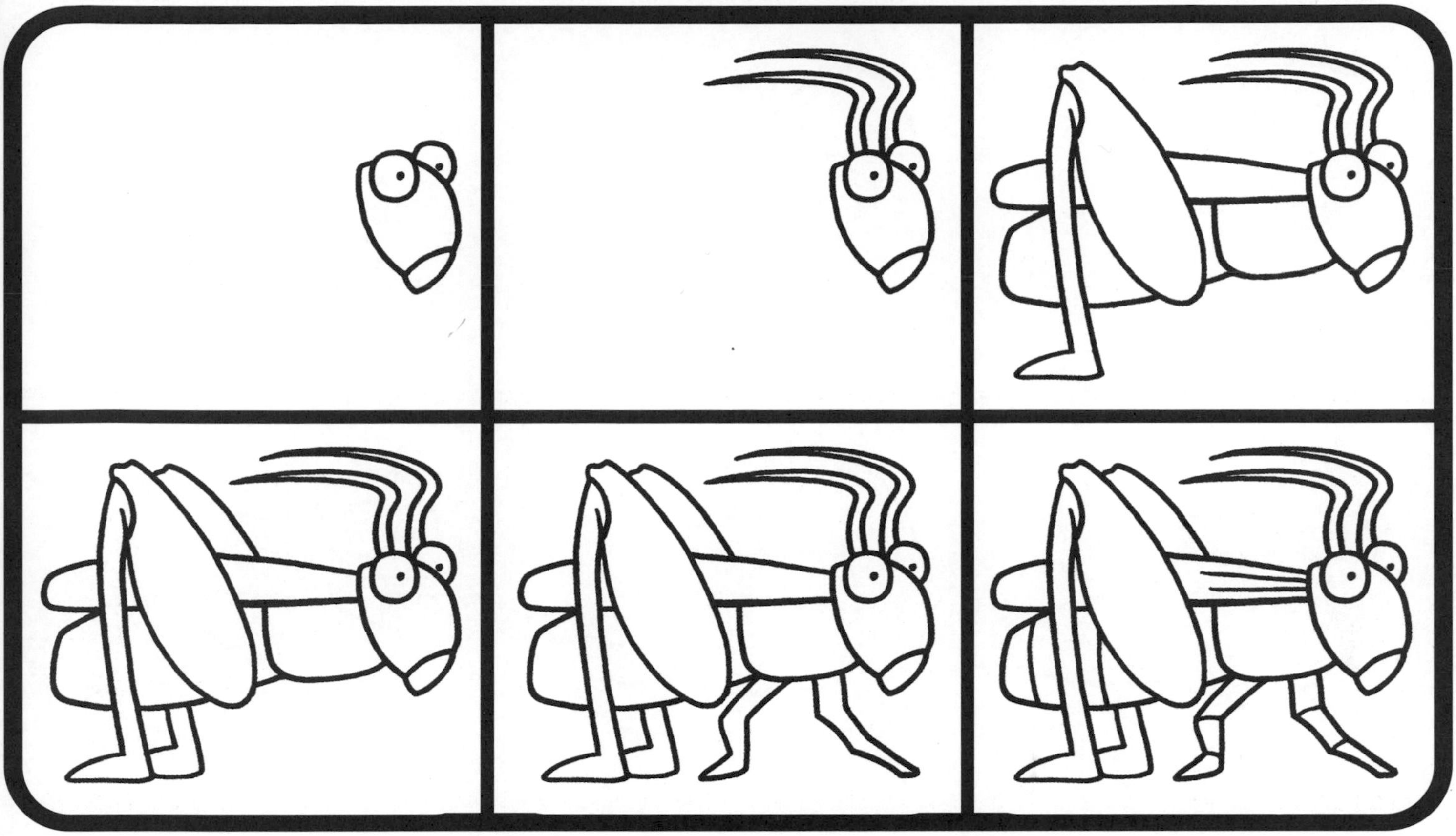

Squid

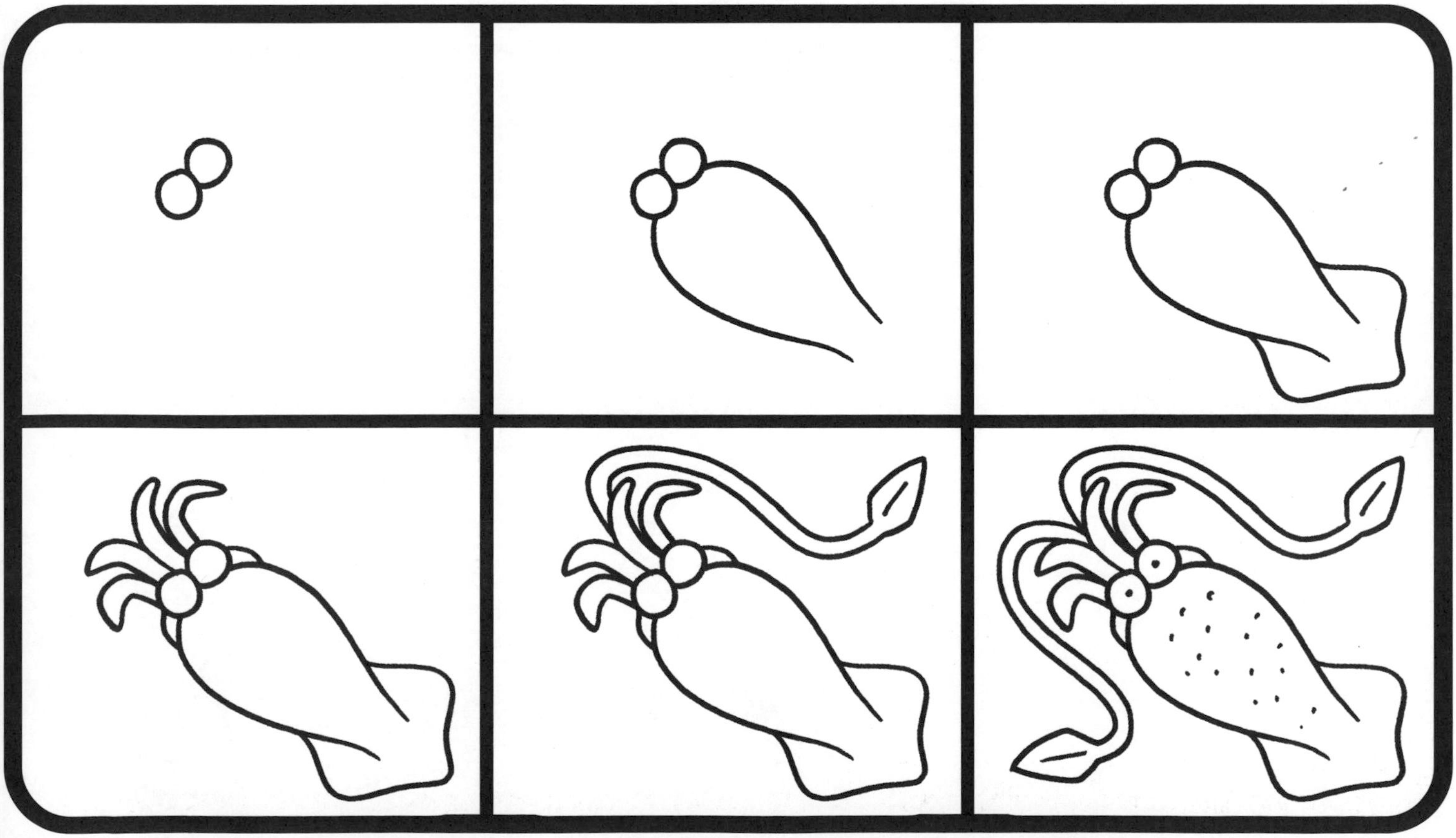

Duck

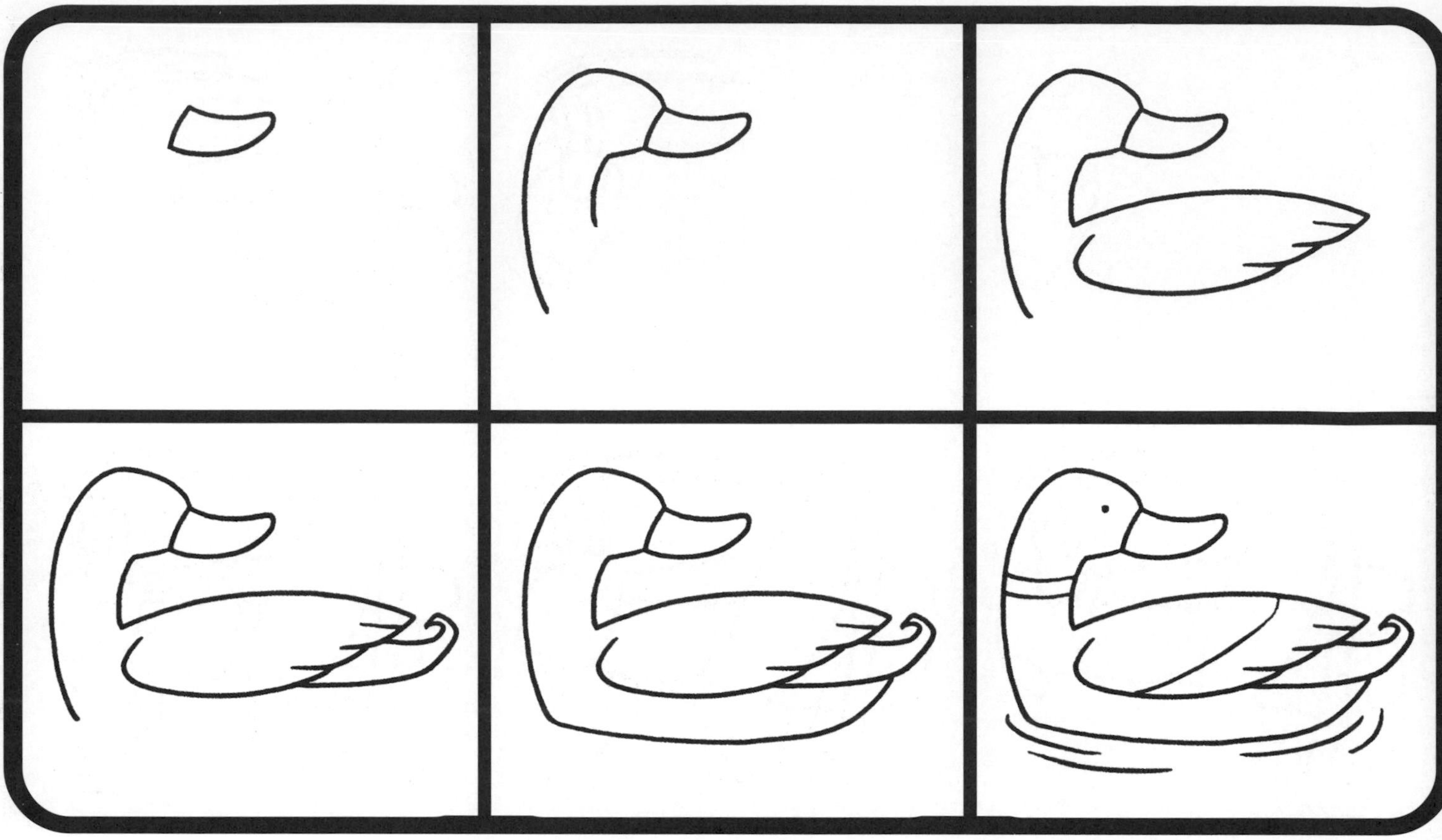

Porcupine

Humpback Whale

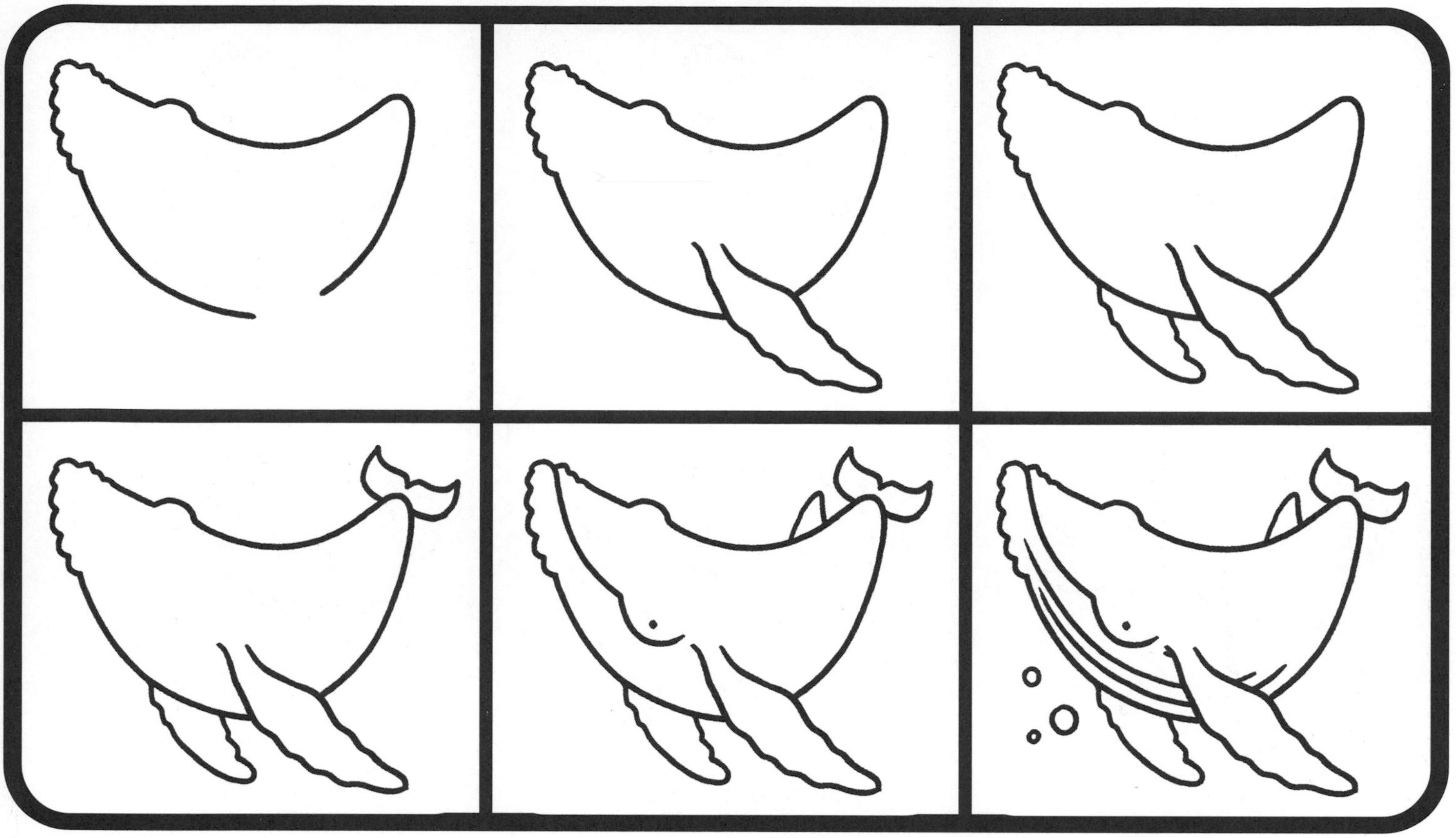

Beaver

Koala

Walrus

Spider

Mouse

Flamingo

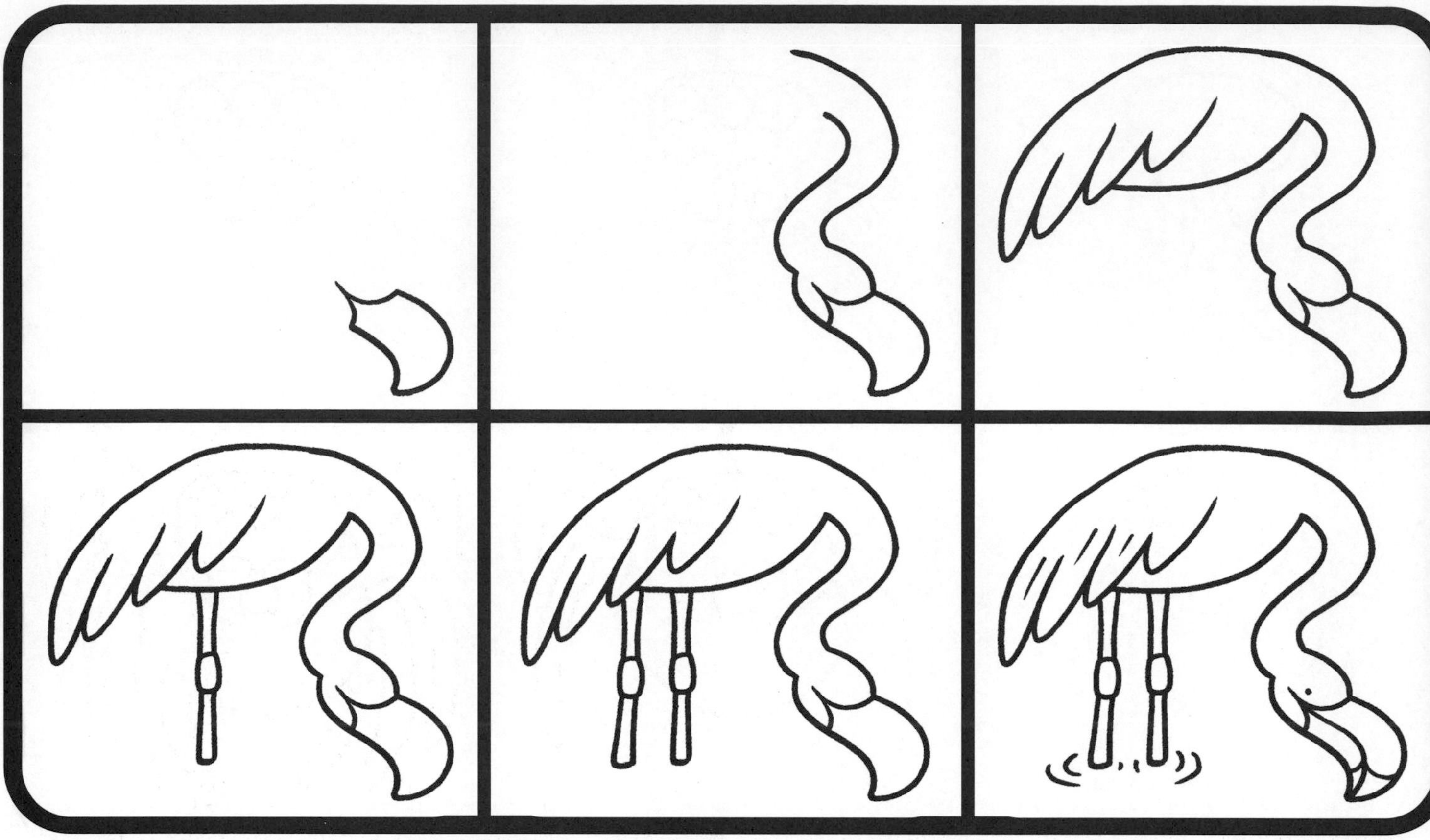

Bear

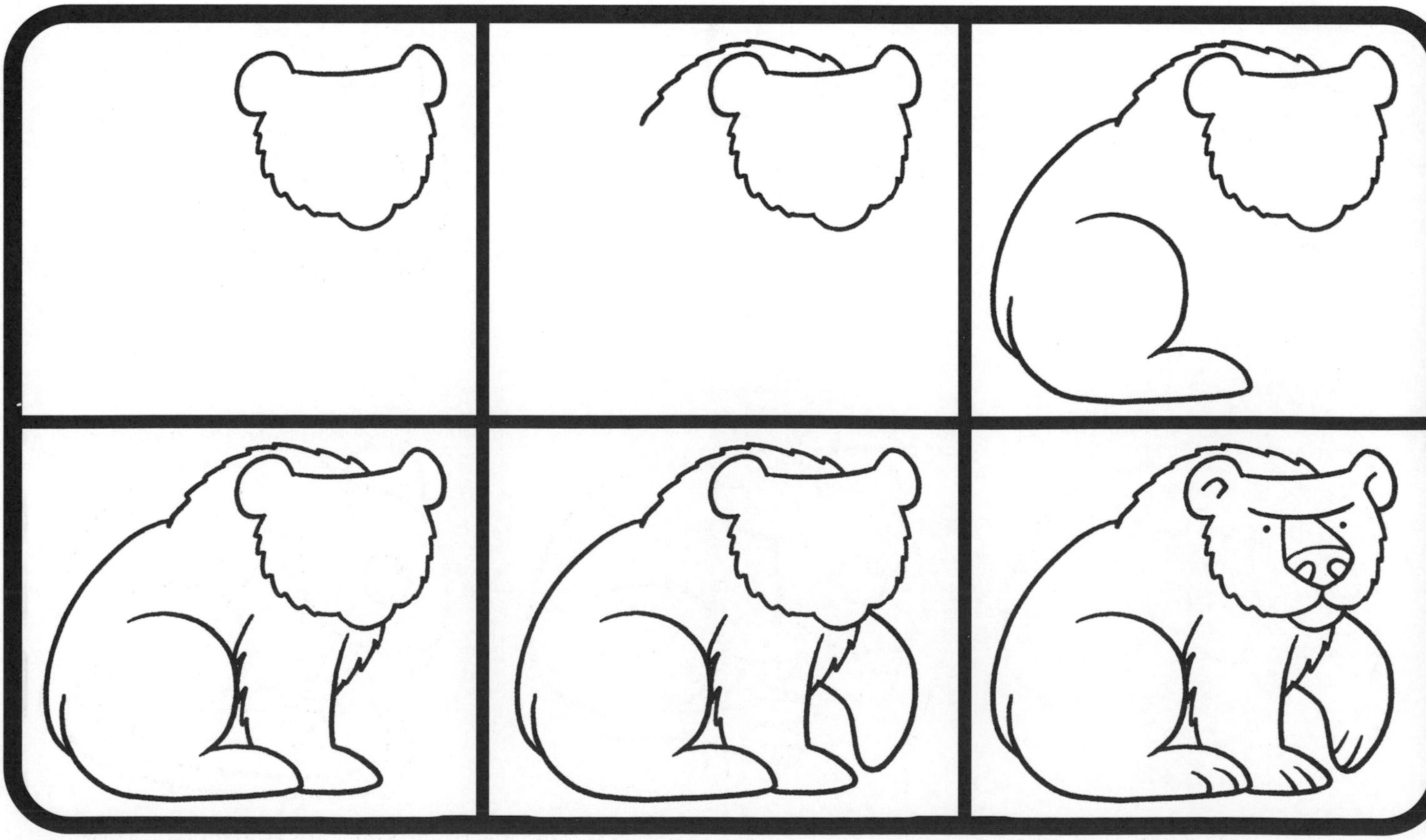

Sloth

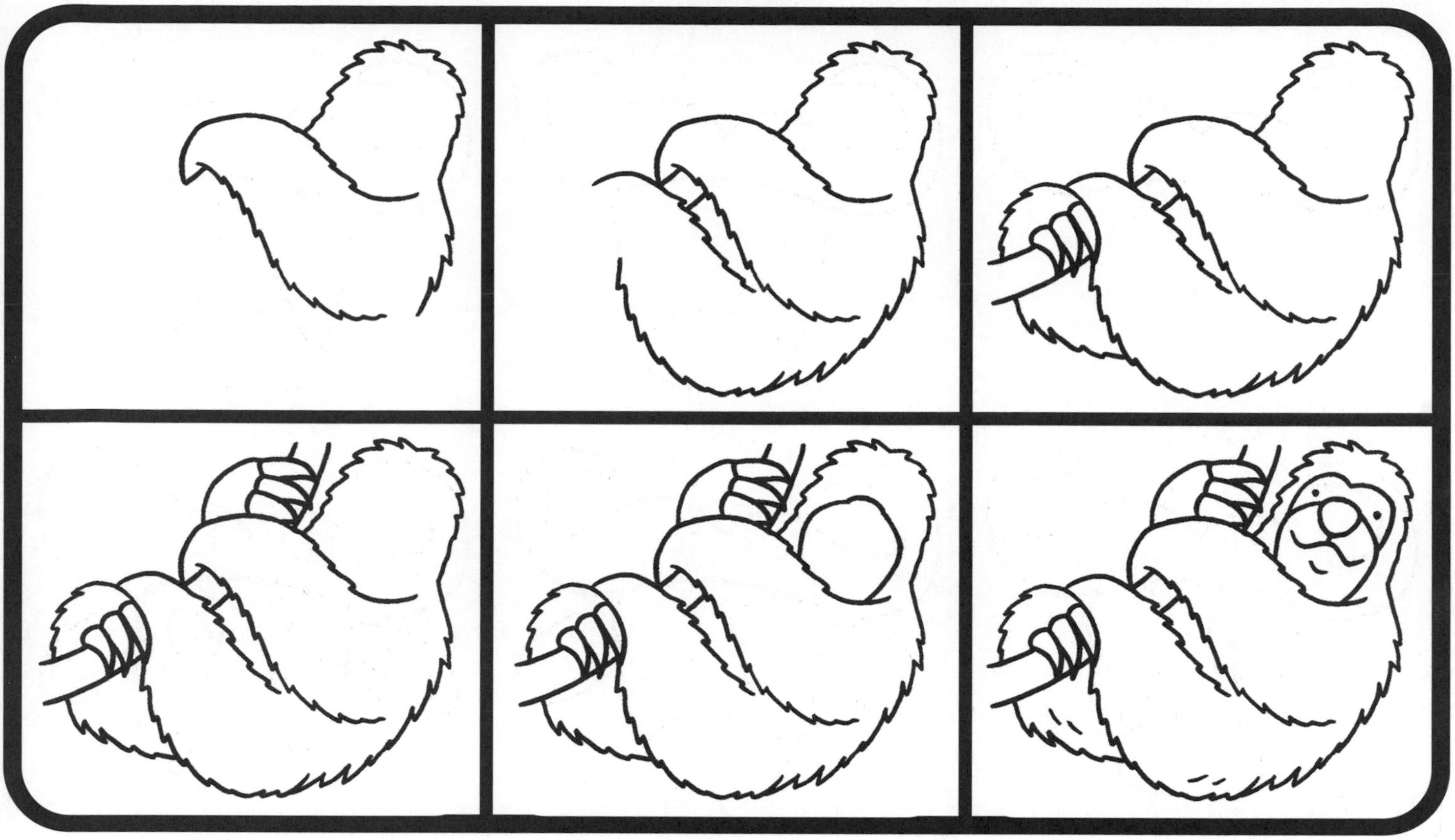

Hippo

Buffalo

Dragonfly

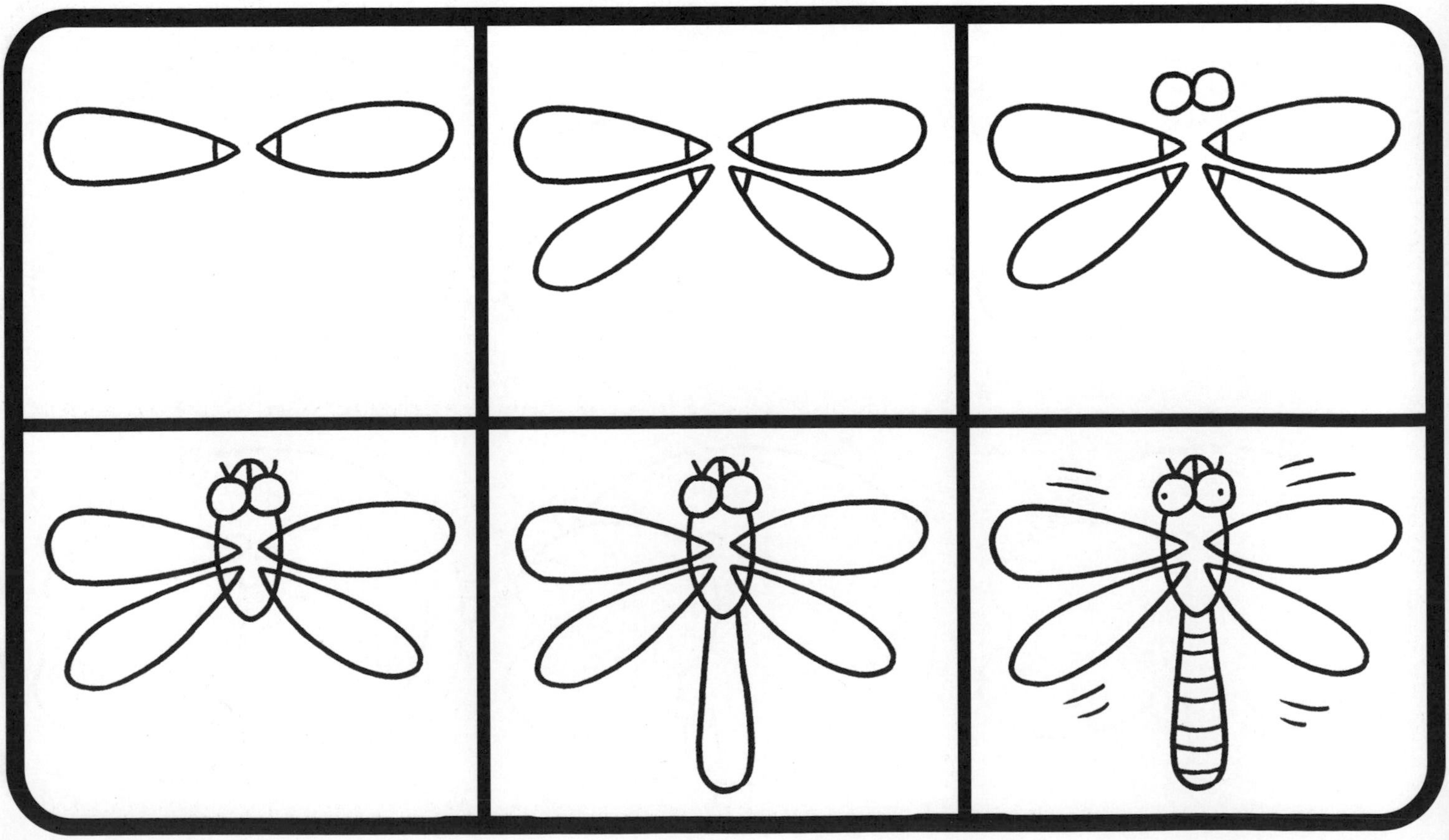

Cheetah

Shrimp

Monkey

Heron

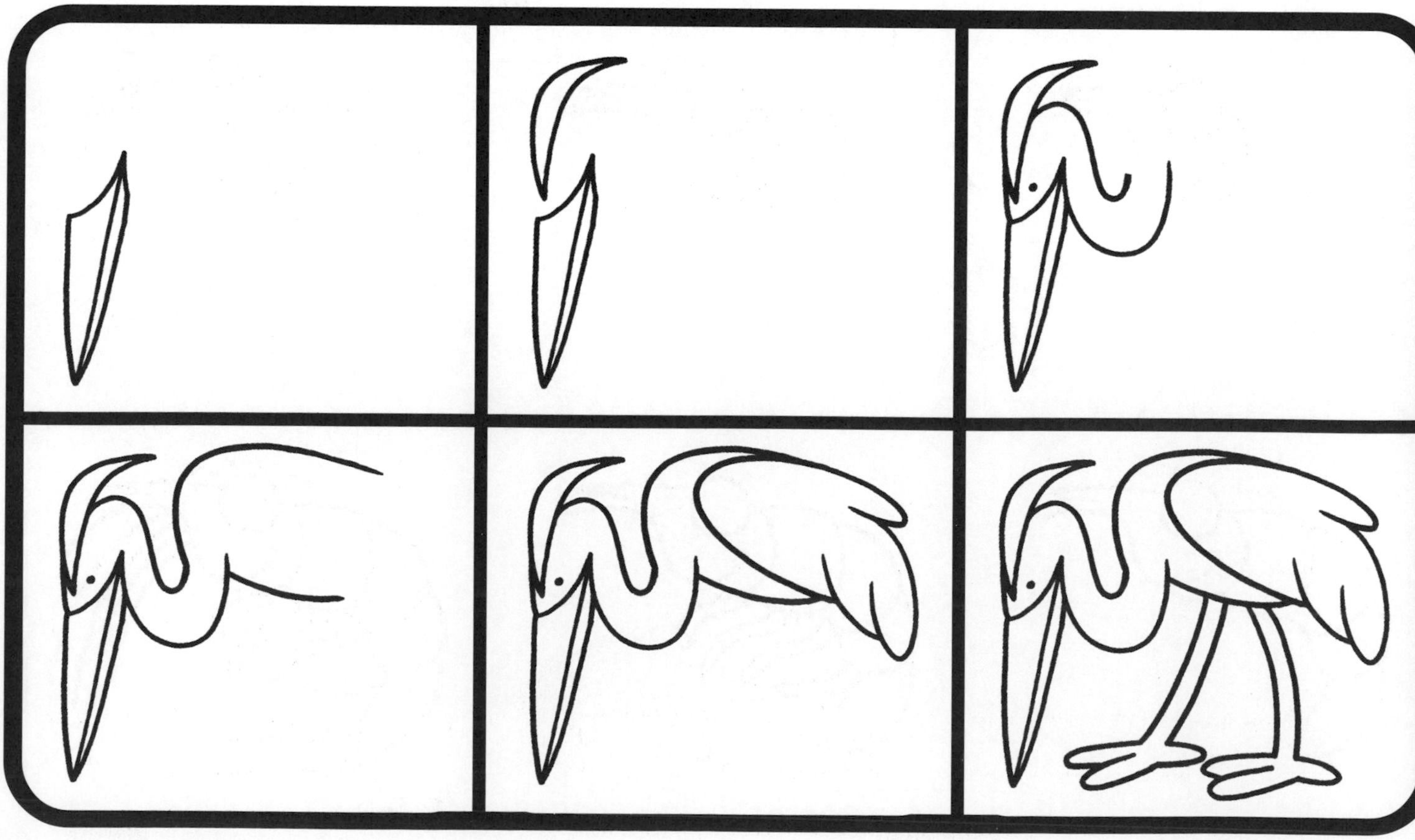

Puffin

Armadillo

octopus

Bee

ostrich

Gorilla

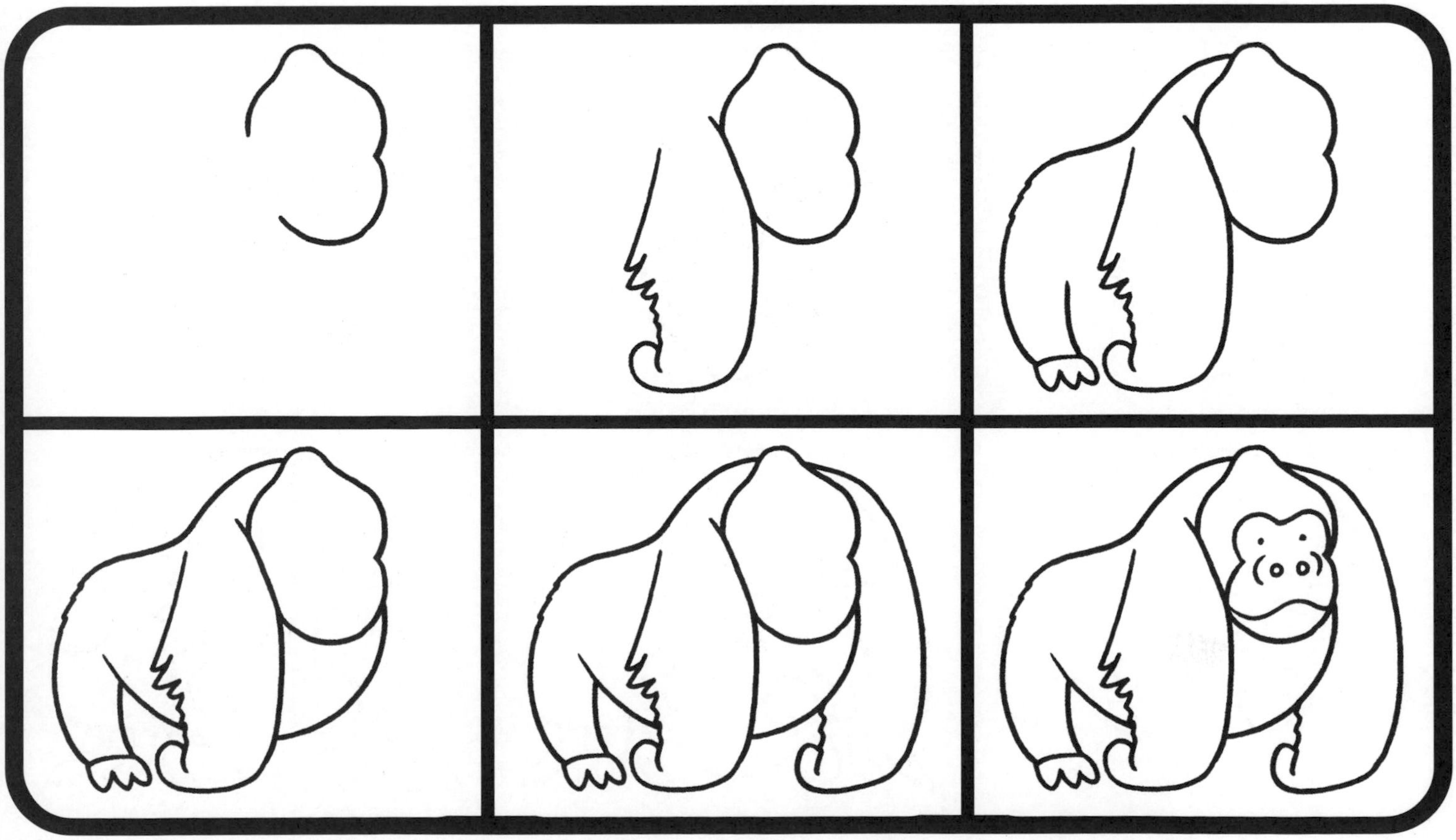

Cuttlefish

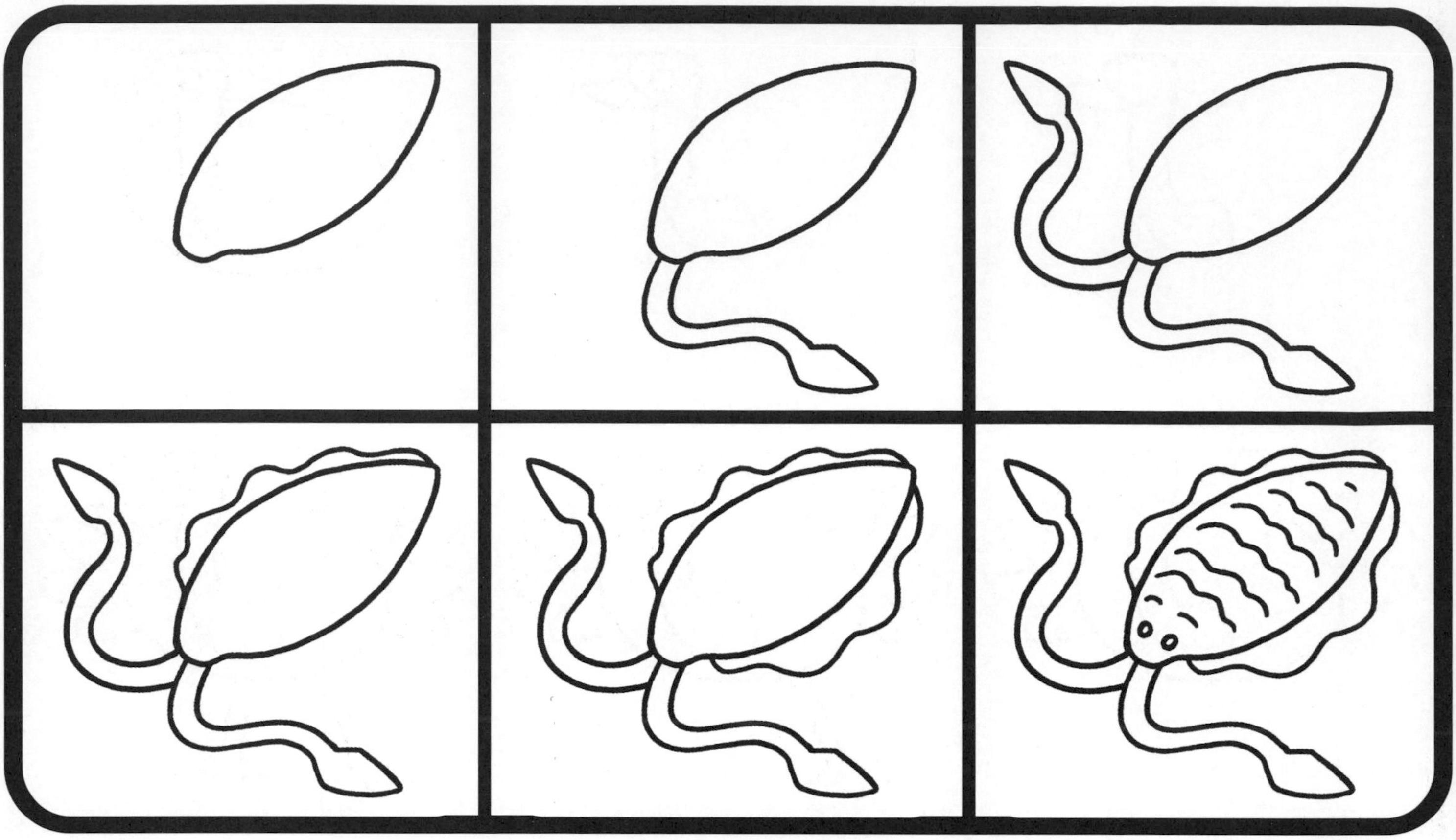

Ladybird

Swan

Manta Ray

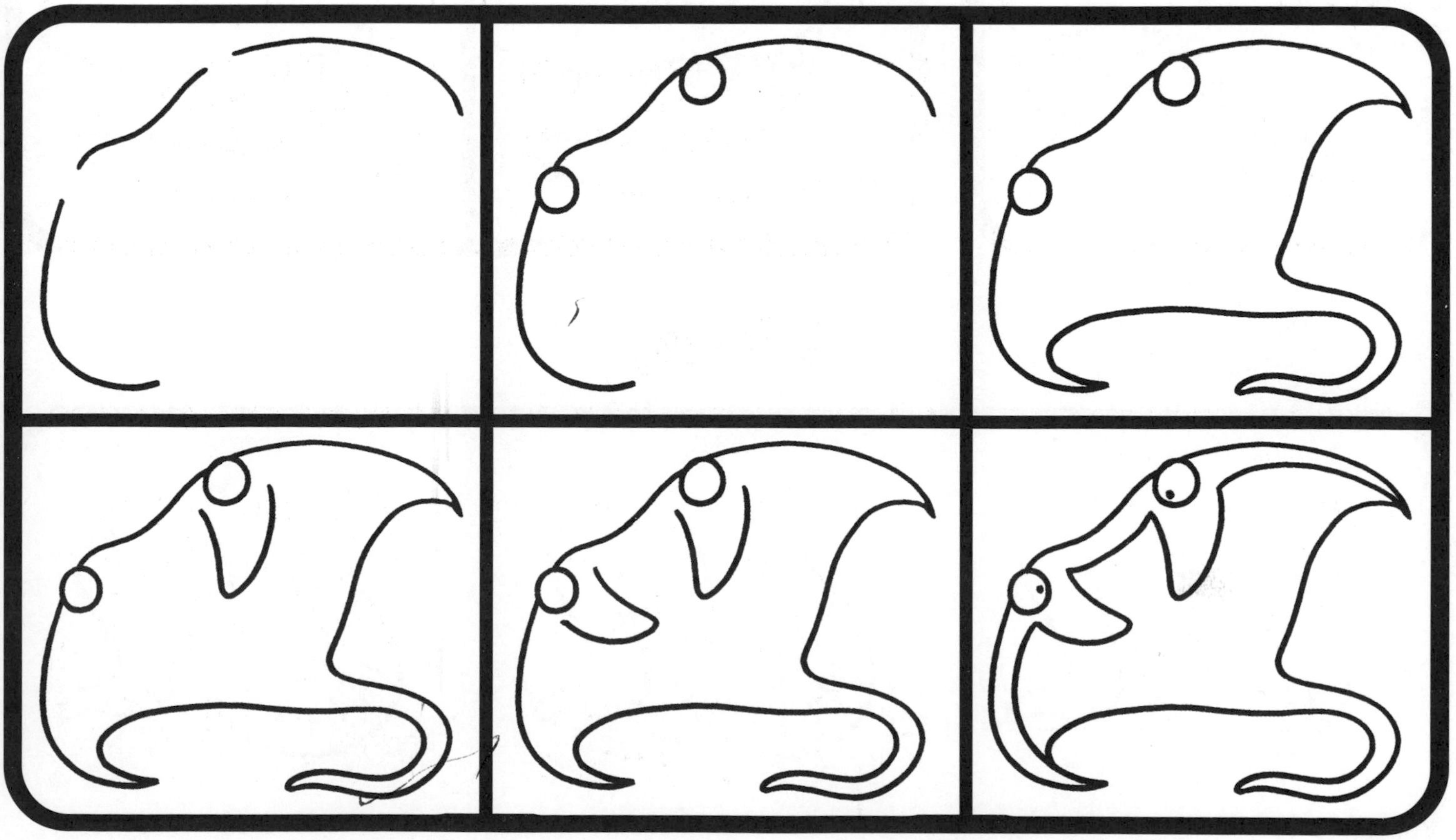

Blue Whale

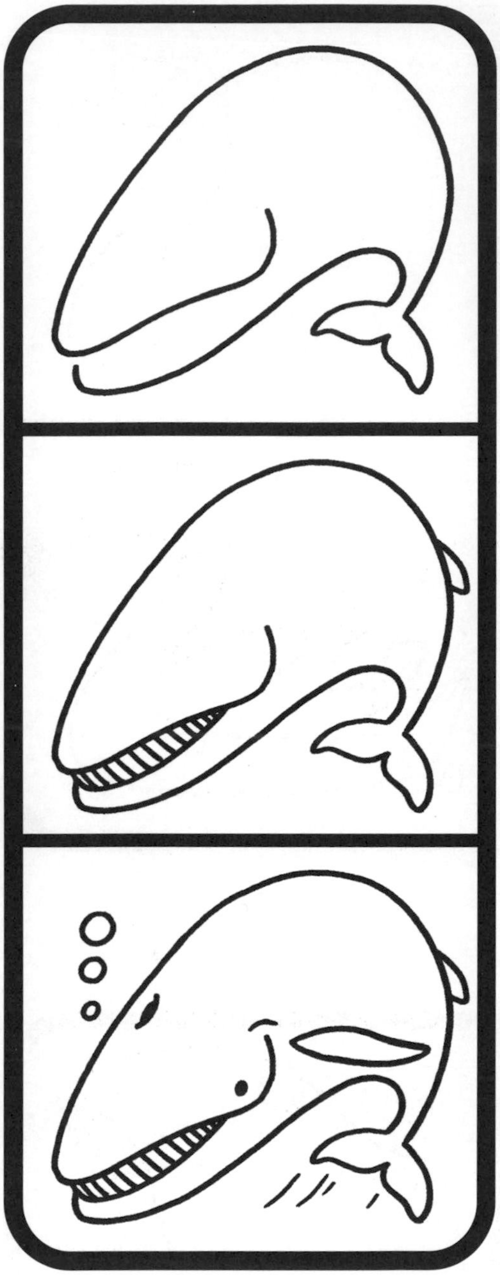

Crocodile

Worm

Wolf

Mole

Angler Fish

Starfish

Polar Bear

Hammerhead Shark

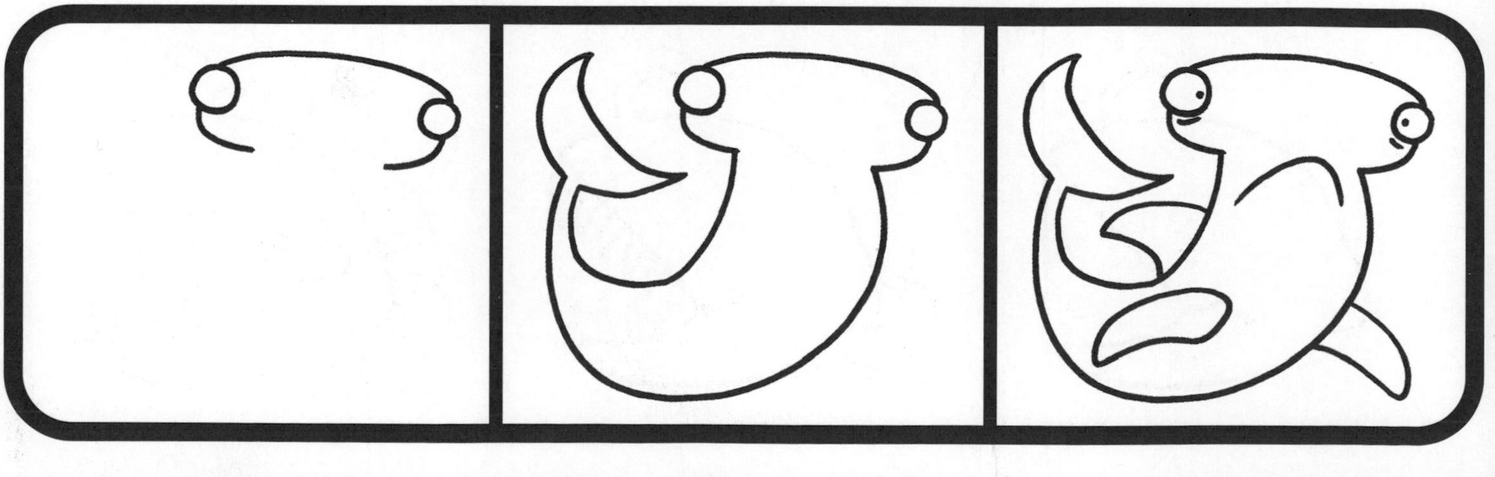

House Fly

Woodpecker

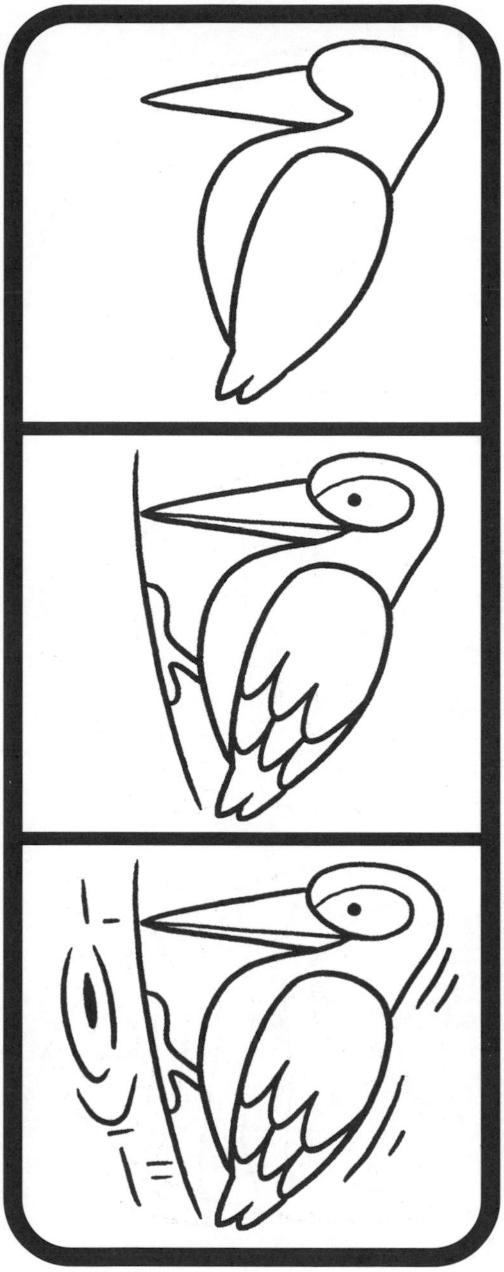

Sperm Whale

Angel Fish

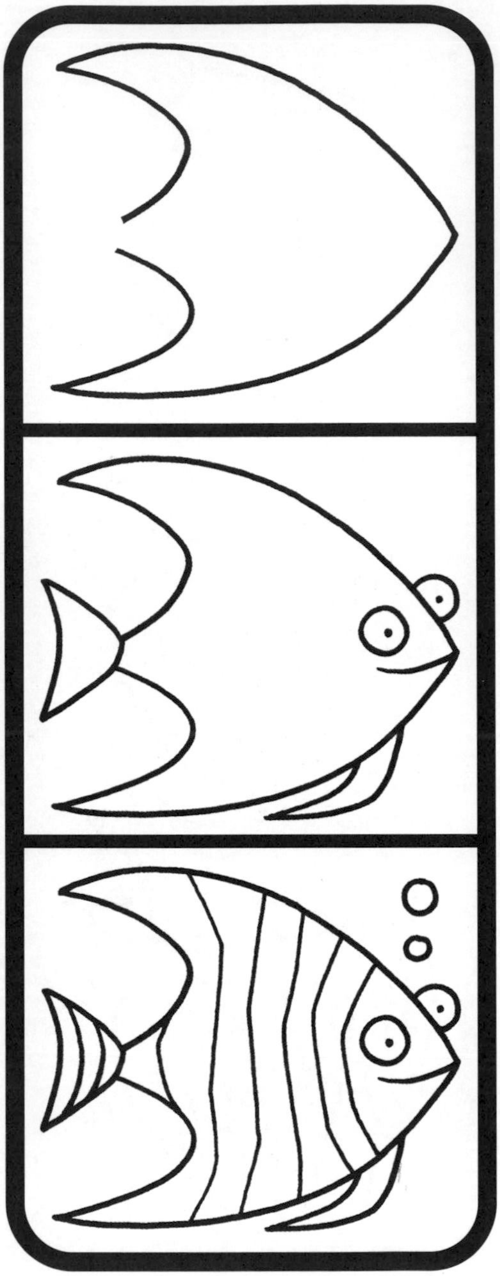

Cobra

Butterfly